The
POWER *of*
JESUS

Sharmila Panirselvam

WESTBOW
PRESS®
A DIVISION OF THOMAS NELSON
& ZONDERVAN

WestBow Press books may be ordered through booksellers or by contacting:

WestBow Press
A Division of Thomas Nelson & Zondervan
1663 Liberty Drive
Bloomington, IN 47403
www.westbowpress.com
844-714-3454

ISBN: 978-1-6642-9953-5 (sc)
ISBN: 978-1-6642-9954-2 (e)

Library of Congress Control Number: 2023908528

Print information available on the last page.

WestBow Press rev. date: 05/19/2023

Contents

Introduction

Jesus is the incarnation of God the Son; Jesus was the awaited Messiah Who walked on earth two thousand years back. He was crucified on the cross, rose again on the third day, and ascended into heaven. He then gave us the Holy Spirit, enabling us to live a powerful Christian life. The Holy Spirit will reveal Jesus, convict us of our sins, draw us closer to God, lead and guide us, endure trials and temptations, and ensure to bring our life into perfection, just like the Lord Jesus Christ. As Christians, we depend on the power of the Holy Spirit that resides in us. When people accept Christ into their hearts, they are born again. Being born again is to experience a new birth in the Spirit. The Lord Jesus said in John 3:3, "Most assuredly, I say to you, unless one is born again, he cannot see the kingdom of God." After that, Jesus went on to say in John 3:5–6, "Most assuredly, I say to you, unless one is born of water and the Spirit, he cannot enter the kingdom of God. That which is born of the flesh is flesh, and that which is born of the Spirit is Spirit." When we are born again in the Spirit, we have the power of Jesus in our lives. Yet, because of the noise, the surrounding circumstance, and the chaos that is going on in this world, we are distracted; in most cases, we ignore that we have God inside us and neglect to acknowledge Him in overcoming every season in this life on earth. Therefore, I have written this book to help newborn Christians to learn more about Jesus and His power, understand the manifestation of the Spirit's power, and exercise it in life.

The Power of Salvation

A postle Paul says in Romans 1:16, "For I am not ashamed of the gospel of Christ, for it is the power of God to salvation for everyone who believes, for the Jew first and also for the Greek."* This verse informs us that whoever believes in the Gospel of Christ will be saved . Jesus is the only-begotten Son of God (John 3:16) Who came to earth, walked among the people, and went to the cross to be slain. Why did this incident happen? Jesus is also called the Lamb of God that took away the world's sins (John 1:29). He became the sin-bearer on the tree on which He hung. Jesus took all our sins in His body on Calvary (1 Peter 2:24).

What is sin, and why are we all sinners in nature? Sin, according to 1 John 3:4, is lawlessness, which in this context means violating God's law, or His commandments. Some would call it rebellion against God. Where did sin start? Sin came from the beginning of the human race; it originates from Adam and Eve in the Garden of Eden. Satan came between Adam and Eve and was the main

---

* Unless otherwise noted, all quotations of scripture come from the New King James Version.

1

character which enticed Eve into sin. How did Satan do that? In the Garden of Eden, God instructed Adam not to eat from one tree, the Tree of the Knowledge of Good and Evil. God warned Adam that the moment he ate from this tree would result in death (Genesis 2:17).

After God created Eve from Adam's rib, a cunning serpent whispered to Eve to eat the fruit from the tree that God had forbidden. The serpent even said, "You will not surely die. For God knows that in the day you eat of it your eyes will be opened, and you will be like God, knowing good and evil" (Genesis 3:4–5). God created Eve as a female companion for a male. The serpent succeeded in convincing Eve, who then took the fruit from the Tree of Knowledge and Evil and ate it. Eve also gave the fruit to Adam to eat. After eating the fruit, their eyes were opened and knew they were naked, immediately covering themselves with fig leaves (Genesis 3:6–7). This is the beginning of the Fall of man or where sin originates in the human race.

The serpent tempted Eve, and Eve fell; Eve believed the serpent and did what she was told. When God knew that Adam and Eve had eaten the fruit, Adam blamed Eve for being the one who gave it to him. God's wrath came upon the serpent, Adam, and Eve, and the Lord God sent them out of Eden (Genesis: 3:23). In Genesis 3:14–15, the Lord cursed the serpent by saying,

> Because you have done this, You are cursed more than all cattle, And more than every beast of the field; On your belly you shall go, and you shall eat dust

> all the days of your life. And I will put
> enmity Between you and the woman,
> And between your seed and her seed;
> He shall bruise your head, And you shall
> bruise His heel.

Then God said to Eve, "I will greatly multiply your sorrow and your conception; In pain, you shall bring forth children; Your desire shall be for your husband, And he shall rule over you" (Genesis 3:16). To Adam, God said:

> Because you have heeded the voice of
> your wife, and have eaten from the tree
> of which I commanded you, saying, "You
> shall not eat of it": Cursed is the ground
> for your sake; In toil, you shall eat of it
> All the days of your life. Both thorns and
> thistles it shall bring forth for you, And
> you shall eat the herb of the field. In the
> sweat of your face, you shall eat bread Till
> you return to the ground, For out of it
> you were taken; For dust you are, And to
> dust, you shall return. (Genesis 3:17–19)

The incident in the Garden of Eden separates human beings from their relationship with God. Since then, every person born into this world has been a sinner in nature. From the scriptures above, you can see why there is so much suffering and pain on this earth; it is a fallen world where the cursed were placed on this earth by God Himself. God's original plan was good: He created Adam and Eve in the image of Himself, knowing no sin

3

and having a relationship with Him and the freedom He gave them. Adam and Eve were then placed in a perfect environment in the Garden. The real reason for God to instruct His first created human not to eat the forbidden tree is to keep humans from knowing evil.

Satan is also called the devil, and the devil is the opposition to God and God's people. Satan hovers over the earth like a roaring lion, seeking to devour anyone, especially God's people. This Satan is in a spirit form we cannot see with our naked eyes. God is also in a spirit form we are not able to see with our naked eyes. Therefore, we must be sober and diligent in differentiating between the Spirit of God and the devil. The devil is ever ready and looking for an opportunity to invade and destroy our lives. Why is Satan after us, the human beings? Satan initially was God's angel, called Lucifer in heaven; Satan wanted to be powerful like God and to sit on the throne of God. When the angel Lucifer wanted to be like God, he was thrown into hell to await God's judgment. When Satan fell from heaven, some angelic host joined Satan and fell concurrently. Revelation 12:9 says, "So the great dragon was cast out, that serpent of old, called the Devil and Satan, who deceives the whole world; he was cast to the earth, and his angels were cast out with him." These angels are also named fallen angels, evil spirits, and demons.

This Satan hovers over this earth to deceive humans because he wants them to be separated from God and to influence people to follow in the footsteps of the fallen angels. These fallen angels were God's creation, but because of their disobedience, they were separated and thrown away from heaven, and now they are constantly disturbing God's people to keep them away from God. These demons are angry because they have been expelled from heaven. The devil is also called the Father of Lies (John 8:44). Satan's job, in short, is to kill, steal, and destroy a person's life (John 10:10).

As a result of Adam and Eve's disobedience, we are all born as sinners, separated from God. When we are separated from God, we are all doomed to go to hell when we die. Anyone who says, "I am not a sinner," is a liar. Why? Even though they may say they have not lied, stolen, fornicated, been drunk, killed, dishonored their parents, or committed adultery, nevertheless, when they say they do not believe in Jesus, the only Son of God, they are condemned (John 3:18). To call someone a "sinner" may sound harsh, but the truth must be preached because Jesus said, "Nobody comes to the Father except through me. I am the way, the life, and the truth" (John 14:6).

The Father sent His Son to earth two thousand years ago to die on the cross and offer forgiveness of sin to humanity. Those who accept Jesus into their heart, believing He died on the cross and rose again on the third day, are restored to God, and they will have eternal life forever in heaven. Even if you are dead on earth, your spirit will be taken to heaven, and you will live with God. Eternal life is promised for those who believe in Jesus (John 3:16). Jesus forgives sins and gives you life—and life more abundantly (1 John 1:9, John 10:10). Once your sins are forgiven, you have new life in Christ. What do you have to do to have this life in Christ? You have to repent of your sins and your iniquities by confessing them through your mouth and then inviting Jesus to come into your heart. A simple salvation prayer can be spoken out loud like this:

> Lord, I know I am a sinner. I confess all my sins. Please forgive me of my sins and iniquities. I believe You died on the cross for my sins, and You rose again on the third day from the dead. I turn away from my past, and I want to walk with You. Lord, please come into my heart. You are my savior and my God. Holy Spirit, please reside in me and lead me into the powerful life as a Christ believer.

Only Jesus can save people from heading to hell. Only Jesus can forgive sin. Therefore, it is wise to repent of our sins and surrender our lives into the hands of the Almighty God. Jesus is the only one with the power to save a life from the wrath of God and His judgment. The power of salvation is in the hands of the one and only God in Christ Jesus. Apart from salvation, we do not have a part in God, and we will not experience the power of God in our lives because Jesus has said we need to be born again to see the kingdom of God. When we are saved by confessing the salvation prayer, we are born again and called children of God (John 3:5–7).

I want to share a little about my salvation story. I was born and raised in a different faith. Since I have a religion, I know I have a God I serve. I constantly talk to God and spend hours praying to get God to talk back. As a little girl at age ten, I sought God fervently because my parents told me God would protect us and care for our life and future. I was very eager for God to show Himself to me. When I was a teenager, I went through a search, and finally, the one true God answered my prayer. It was weird because I know Jesus but was never taught He is an actual living God Who will answer my call. I encountered the living God in a Pentecostal church. The Gospel preached by the pastor and the overwhelming heat that went through my body was an authentic encounter with God. The preaching of God's Word was powerful and penetrated my heart, and the touch of the presence of heat assured me that God is here on earth. Ever since that encounter, the rest is history. Jesus is the one true God with the power to save the people from perishing.

The Power of Transformation

J esus holds the power of life transformation in His
hands. The moment we are born again, the Holy Spirit
will convict us with our sins. The Holy Spirit will nudge
us to do the right thing. Why? Because the Holy Spirit
is the Spirit of Jesus. The Holy Spirit is God, and He is
holy. Our God is three in One: the Heavenly Father, the
Lord Jesus, and the Holy Spirit. The Heavenly Father
and the Lord Jesus are in heaven and not on earth. Jesus
said in John 16:7, "Nevertheless, I tell you the truth. It
is to your advantage that I go away; for if I do not go
away, the Helper will not come to you; but if I depart, I
will send Him to you." When Jesus rose again from His
death and ascended to heaven, He did not leave us like a
sheep without the shepherd. He gave us the Holy Spirit to
continually have a close intimate relationship with God.

When we are continually aware that the Holy Spirit
is in us, we are inclined towards the holiness of God.
Even though our flesh will still desire to do ungodly
things, eventually, we will be guided and brought back
into the right path. Transformation happens a little at a
time. Ask God to reveal any crooked way in you, and ask
Him to guide you into holiness. In Psalm 139:23–24, the

Psalmist says, "Search me, O God, and know my heart; Try me, and know my anxieties; And see if there is any wicked way in me, And lead me in the way everlasting." Perfection is achieved when we see Jesus face to face when we leave this earth.

The Holy Spirit invades every facet of our lives, and the purity spills over in nearly everything we do daily. The way we treat people, handle our finances, do our job, and take care of our health, and our educational pursuits will all be inclined towards purity. We will see every part of our life through the lens of spirituality. The Holy Spirit's presence will make us seek first the kingdom of God and His righteousness, and everything else shall be added into our lives (Matthew 6:33). The love for God is increased, and when we love our Savior so much, we will want to please God rather than do what the world can offer.

Jesus does not want us to be conformed to this world but to be transformed by renewing the mind so we may prove what God's good and acceptable and perfect will is (Romans 12:2). Therefore, reading the Word of God daily is crucial to ensure we know what is right and wrong. When we do what is right, we please God; we walk as obedient children to God and ultimately experience the blessing of God on this earth. Doing the right thing takes practice. As long as we desire to be with Jesus and follow Him, the Holy Spirit in us will help us towards a godly life.

When we read the Word of God daily, we will be reminded by many scriptures that guide and lead us into the path the Lord had prepared for us in this. As for me, the scripture from Galatians 2:20 resonates with me because of my love for Jesus. Galatians 2:20 says, "I have been crucified with Christ; it is no longer I who live, but Christ lives in me; and the life which I now live in the flesh I live by faith in the Son of God, who loved me and gave Himself for me." Therefore, my life and the desires of my heart, I gave into my living God's hands, and whatever He wants me to do, I will do it. I live a surrendered life, calling my life a living sacrifice.

You may ask what a surrendered life is; what is a living sacrifice? An example of a surrendered life is what Jesus said in John 6:28: "For I have come down from heaven, not to do My own will, but the will of Him who sent Me." Even though Jesus is God 100 percent and man 100 percent, He surrendered His will into the hands of the Heavenly Father. Whatever the Heavenly Father wanted Him to do on earth, He did it. It is the same for us when we live a surrendered life. For us, we should seek the Lord fervently and ask Him what He wants us to accomplish on this earth. The Holy Spirit will never fail to lead in that direction that leads to the Heavenly Father's will for us in this lifetime.

Meanwhile, a "living sacrifice," according to apostle Paul, in Romans 12:1, says, "I beseech you therefore, brethren, by the mercies of God, that you present your bodies a living sacrifice, holy, acceptable to God, which is your reasonable service." In this context, Apostle Paul says to present your life as a service to God. We do this by not conforming to the pattern of this world. The world is living through the lust of the flesh, which we crave to have riches, fame, beauty, power, sex, and many more things. According to the Bible in Matthew 6:26, scripture says, "For what profit is it to a man if he gains the whole world, and loses his soul? Or what will a man give in exchange for his soul?"

When we have everything we need through the lust of our flesh but do not have eternal life with God, we gain nothing. All the sweat we put in earning everything we wanted on earth will not be an inherited blessing to the next generation. A blessed life comes from obedience to God. We can still become rich, famous, and powerful by following God's way, but the difference is, we will leave a blessed legacy behind. When we do it in God's way, we do not lie, cheat, steal, or kill to be rich and famous, but we obey the precepts of God, and God will honor that. Yet, you may say many people had become billionaires without being wicked, but the point here is, you missed eternal life.

To dive a little deeper, being a living sacrifice is like offering our entire body, mind, and soul to God. Our body is the temple of the Holy Spirit (1 Corinthians 6:19). Therefore, we should not abuse our bodies with unholy things. Corrupt things are like having sex out of marriage, being drunk, listening and watching stuff that is destructive to our future. 1 Corinthians 6:9–10 said, "Do you not know that the unrighteous will not inherit the kingdom of God? Do not be deceived. Neither fornicators, nor idolaters, nor adulterers, nor homosexuals, nor sodomites, nor thieves, covetous, drunkards, nor revilers, nor extortioners will inherit the kingdom of God". These corrupt things may have been in our life before, but when we receive Christ, we have the Holy

Spirit in us. Therefore, it is critically important how we conduct our lives. It seems like a restricted life, but life in the Spirit of God is a life of abundance and freedom. There is freedom where the Spirit of the Lord is (2 Corinthians 3:17), and Jesus said He had come to give us life and life more abundantly (John 10:10).

It is for our good to follow the teachings of Jesus, and you will see the fruit in every aspect of your life. This does not mean we will not go through trials, tribulations, and the ups and downs of daily life; when Jesus is in us, He will help us endure every season with grace, and victory is on our side. Many things will follow in the way that the Lord wants you to walk on this earth. When we know Jesus is with us through His Holy Spirit, our minds must be taught to think about good and holy things. Our feelings also should be tuned in to what is acceptable and pleasant to God. It seems like a difficult task to achieve this state of mind and emotion. Still, one can do it by daily reading the Word of God, praying and seeking God, worshiping Him, praising Him, listening to the Word of God being preached by a man of God like a pastor, attending Bible study, and attending church every Sunday to gather with other saints in prayer.

To summarize, Jesus holds the power to transform one life while living on this earth. When we repent and are born again, we will learn to let go of the past and walk into the new. We start as baby Christians when we are newly born again, and as life goes on, we are gradually being molded and mature, and we will be valuable vessels for the Lord Jesus. As long as we abide in Christ, like the scripture from John 15:4–6, Jesus says, "Abide in Me, and

I in you. As the branch cannot bear fruit of itself unless it abides in the vine, neither can you, unless you abide in Me, I am the vine, you are the branches. He who abides in Me, and I in him, bears much fruit; you can do nothing without Me. If anyone does not abide in Me, he is cast out as a branch and is withered; they gather them and throw them into the fire, and they are burned." When we abide in Jesus, we can see the fruit of the Spirit in our daily conduct, which includes love, joy, peace, long-suffering, kindness, goodness, faithfulness, gentleness, and self-control (Galatians 5:22–23). Long-suffering here refers to being patient in trials and tribulations.

As the Spirit changes us over time, and from glory to glory, we are transformed into the image of Christ. The Word of God from 2 Corinthians 3:18 says, "But we all, with unveiled face, beholding as in a mirror the glory of the Lord, are being transformed into the same image from glory to glory, just as by the Spirit of the Lord." Want to have a transformed life? Submit your life to Jesus, let Him take authority over your life, and monitor the change you will experience.

The Power of the Word

The Word of God is powerful because it is Spirit and life (John 6:63). The Word of God in the Bible can perform and accomplish the task that God intended to achieve. Therefore, beware, do not disrespect the Word of God. The Word of God must be put at the highest place in the life of a believer. Why is that so? Because every Word in the Bible is God's breath. The author of the Bible is God, and God used men led by the Holy Spirit to write the scriptures. When the Holy Spirit guided these authors, they wrote under the direct direction of God Himself. Furthermore, in 2 Timothy 3:16, the Bible says, "All Scripture is given by inspiration of God, and is profitable for doctrine, for reproof, for correction, for instruction in righteousness."

The Bible is a guide for a Christian. The entire Bible is about Jesus. The Old Testament points to Jesus and His coming as a Messiah. The New Testament is when Jesus walked on earth. Every word in the Bible must be paid attention to. The Word is the power unto human salvation (2 Corinthians 11:23–26). When someone preaches the Gospel, and people get saved, that is the power of the Gospel or the Word of God. Christians should read the Bible daily to grow in their faith. Daily reading of the Word is the key to knowing the ways and mind of Christ. Why does change take place? It is because there is power in the Word of God. On top of that, faith is built by reading and listening to the Word of God daily. When faith becomes more robust, the surrounding circumstances have less power to influence us. Therefore, it is crucial to immerse ourselves in the Word of God.

The Word of God should be kept hidden in the heart of a Christian. Hebrews 4:12 says, "For the word of God is living and powerful, and sharper than any two-edged sword, piercing even to the division of soul and spirit, and joints and marrow, and is a discerner of the thoughts and intents of the heart." As Christians, we have spiritual enemies. These spiritual enemies include the devil, or Satan. Do you remember the time when Adam and Eve sinned against God? They were tempted by the serpent; in other words, the devil tempted them. Since then, we know we have a very close enemy ready to devour us. John 10:10 says, "The thief comes only to kill, steal and destroy." The thief is also referred to as Satan.

An excellent example is to learn from Jesus our Lord how He resists the devil. I will put the entire scripture below from Matthew 4:1–11:

> Then, the Spirit led Jesus into the wilderness to be tempted by the devil. After fasting for forty days and forty nights, he was hungry. The tempter came to him and said, "If you are the Son of God, tell these stones to become bread."

Jesus answered, "It is written: 'Man shall not live on bread alone, but on every word that comes from the mouth of God.' Then the devil took him to the holy city and had him stand on the temple's highest point. "If you are the Son of God," he said, "throw yourself down. For it is written: "He will command his angels concerning you, and they will lift you in their hands so that you will not strike your foot against a stone.' Jesus answered, "It is also written: 'Do not put the Lord your God to the test.' Again, the devil took him to a very high mountain and showed him all the kingdoms of the world and their splendor. "All this I will give you," he said, "if you will bow down and worship me." Jesus said to him, "Away from me, Satan! It is written: 'Worship the Lord your God and serve him only. Then the devil left him, and angels came and attended him.

Do you see how Jesus defeated the enemy with words? We should be as sharp as Jesus; Jesus came to save us from going to eternal fire after death, but He also showed us how to defeat Satan on earth at every level, using the power of words. To ensure we are clear on why the Word of God is powerful when we speak it out, is because we have the living God in us, the Holy Spirit. The Holy Spirit in us makes the Word of God live. Therefore, the Word of God is capable of casting out Satan and destroying every attempt of Satan. We will fight Satan throughout our lives, and victory is in our sight because Jesus and His words are a powerful weapon that kills the works of Satan. We who live in the flesh can be tempted every day and at every phase of our lives, but never forget, we have the Word of God to overcome it.

Here is another example to show you the power of words. Our Heavenly Father is the creator. He created heaven and earth. How did He do that? He did it by speaking out about what He wanted to create. Let me put the scripture below from Genesis 1:3–9, so you can read what the Lord God said at the very beginning, before humans were created, even before the earth was formed:

> Then God said, "Let there be light,"; and there was light. And God saw the light, that it was good; and God divided the light from the darkness. God called the light day, and the darkness He called night. So the evening and the morning were the first days.

> Then God said, "Let there be a firmament amid the waters, and let it divide the waters from the waters." Thus, God made the firmament and divided the waters which were under the firmament from the waters which were above the firmament; and it was so. And God called

the firmament Heaven. So the evening and the morning were the second days.

Then God said, "Let the waters under the heavens be gathered together into one place, and let the dry land appear,"; and it was so. And God called the dry land Earth, and the gathering together of the waters He called Seas. And God saw that it was good.

Then God said, "Let there be lights in the firmament of the heavens to divide the day from the night, and let them be for signs and seasons, and days and years, and let them be for lights in the firmament of the heavens to give light on the earth"; and it was so. Then God made two great lights: the greater light to rule the day and the lesser light to rule the night. He made the stars also. God set them in the firmament of the heavens to give light on the earth, rule over the Day and the Night, and divide the light from the darkness. And God saw that it was good. So the evening and the morning were the fourth days.

Did you see the words "God said" each time the Heavenly Father wanted to create something new? In Psalm 33:6, the scripture says, "By the Word of the Lord the heavens were made, And all the host of them by the breath of His mouth." On Day One, the Lord said, "Let there be light, and there was light"; by the power of the

Word, the Lord created the light. Heaven and earth were spoken words by the Heavenly Father, and it appears.

Now let's see one more example of how Jesus used the power of the Word to make things happen. The example can be seen here from Mark 11:20–24:

> Now in the morning, they saw the fig tree dried up from the roots as they passed by. And Peter, remembering, said to Him, "Rabbi, look! The fig tree which You cursed has withered away."
>
> So Jesus answered and said to them, "Have faith in God. For assuredly, I say to you. Whoever says to this mountain, 'Be removed and be cast into the sea,' and does not doubt in his heart but believes that those things he says will be done, he will have whatever he says. Therefore, I say to you, whatever things you ask when you pray, believe that you receive them, and you will have them."

The example above confirms that Jesus spoke a word to the fig tree, and the fig tree faded away. Then Jesus said you must have faith when you say something; It will be done for you. Then Jesus said to believe whatever we ask in prayer to have faith in that prayer, and we will have them. When our faith is combined with the spoken Word, the Word will not return void. Words have power. How does the Word have power? Well, it is because of the Holy Spirit in us that makes the Word powerful.

I must clarify that the scripture above is God Himself speaking the Word into existence, making things die or be alive. There are things that only God can do, but what about us, humans? Well, God has given us the scripture, the Word of God in the Bible, for us to read and gain understanding, and we can employ the written Word of God and say it out loud in every circumstance we face. In any given situation, look for the appropriate scripture, and say it aloud. Talk to God about your situation, and ask for wisdom in every life issue that comes your way. Give time for God to show you the way; eventually, you will know what to do and overcome it. God works in mysterious ways; our human brains are too small to know all of God's thoughts.

Proverbs 18:21 says, "Death and life are in the power of the tongue, And those who love it will eat its fruit." Therefore, speak words that can build and give life to others. Speaking negative words can cause negative effects; therefore, speak whatever is good and positive towards others and yourself. The mouth is meant to speak words that give hope, life, strength, and courage. As you speak in such a way, you will move towards a life God prepared for you on this earth.

In conclusion, as a child of God, spoken words have the power to build or destroy you. Beware what you speak, choose the right words, and think before you speak. It is a good practice to read the Bible out loud. In my daily reading, I read in silence and aloud as well. The scriptures can change how I live my life and ultimately produce the right actions that are godly. Jesus has made us have power in the spoken word.

The Power of Faith

According to the Bible, faith is the substance of things hoped for, the evidence of things not seen (Hebrews 11:1). I want you to understand what this means. Let me give you another scripture that Jesus taught us in Mark 11:24: "Therefore I say to you, whatever things you ask when you pray, believe that you receive them, and you will have them." Thus, faith is putting trust in God in everything, while hope is believing in the future that God will perform it. Believing it will happen in the future is something you don't see right now, but you trust God that He will bring it to pass.

Another scripture from 2 Corinthians 5:7 says, "For we walk by faith, not by sight." Following Jesus means we have dedicated ourselves to living on the spiritual path God had prepared for us. We cannot see or touch things in the spiritual realm when we live spiritually. It is the same with the Holy Spirit you cannot see or touch the Holy Spirit, but you believe and trust that the Holy Spirit abides in you once you are saved. It is called living in faith when you believe and trust in God and His words in the Bible.

You trust God for every promise in the Bible, and you stand on the promise that it will come to pass according to the timing of God. You don't doubt the Word of God and His existence, even when you don't feel it, but instead, trust, believe, and obey Him. This is called faith; your conduct is based on the Bible's teachings, and you have confidence it will produce blessings in the future. In short, faith is your dependency on God in this lifetime on earth. In every aspect of life, have faith He will lead, guide, and accomplish everything He wants you to do; even in good times and bad times, you know you can hold on to Jesus, and He will never disappoint you; eventually, triumph is on your side.

Now, why is faith powerful? I want to bring you back to the scripture where Jesus cursed the fig tree in Mark 11:14. The next day, Jesus's disciples found the tree Jesus cursed withered away. With unbelief seeing it with their eyes, the disciples told Jesus the tree had died. In response, Jesus replied, "Have faith in God. For assuredly, I say to you; whoever says to this mountain, 'Be removed and be cast into the sea,' and does not doubt in his heart but believes that those things he says will be done, he will have whatever he says" (Mark 11:22–23). When you read further, you will find that Jesus also said, "Therefore I say to you, whatever things you ask when you pray, believe that you receive them, and you will have them" (Mark 11:24).

The above is the teaching from Jesus to the disciples that they should have faith and not doubt, so whatever they ask for it, they will receive it. I learned from here that God is pleased with our faith in Him. God knows our hearts because one of His attributes is being omniscient; He is all-knowing. Therefore, He knows our thoughts and our heart. God knows when you have faith and delight in Him, and He will work it out according to your good. You also must remember God answers prayer and helps you grow in faith and ultimately transforms your life. If you don't get what you request or ask, it simply means God wants you to stay away from it because it harms you and your future. Sometimes, some prayer takes time because God has appointed a time for everything. The point is to have faith, and you will move mountains with God. When you have faith in what God can do for you, you will move forward and never be stagnant.

Let me share another scripture explaining why faith is powerful. This scripture is from Matthew 14:28–31:

> And Peter answered Him and said, "Lord, if it is You, command me to come to You on the water." So He said, "Come." And when Peter came down off the boat, he walked on water to go to Jesus. But when he saw that the wind was boisterous, he was afraid; and beginning to sink, he cried out, saying, "Lord, save me!" And immediately, Jesus stretched out His hand, caught him, and said, "O you of little faith, why did you doubt?"

Jesus once again taught His disciples to have faith. The moment you doubt it, that displeases God, and nothing happens. Faith is crucially needed in following Jesus because faith is a tool that Jesus Himself repeatedly told His disciples to exercise.

It is wise to obey what Jesus is teaching in the Bible because there is where the power is found. Let me show you another example from the scripture on faith. The scripture is in Mark 9:17–23:

Then one of the crowd answered, "Teacher, I brought You my son, who has a mute spirit. And wherever it seizes him, it throws him down; he foams at the mouth, gnashes his teeth, and becomes rigid. So I spoke to Your disciples, that they should cast it out, but they could not." He answered and said, "O faithless generation, how long shall I be with you? How long shall I bear with you? Bring him to Me." Then they brought him to Him. And when he saw Him, immediately the Spirit convulsed him, and he fell on the ground and wallowed, foaming at the mouth. So He asked his Father, "How long has this been happening to him?" And he said, "From childhood. And often, he has thrown him both into the fire and into the water to destroy him. But if You can do anything, have compassion on us and help us." Jesus said to him, "If you can believe, all things are possible to him who believes." Immediately the father of the child cried out and said with tears, "Lord, I believe; help my unbelief!" Once again Jesus is teaching us to have faith in Him the Son of God that He can cast out the unclean spirit and to heal the sick.

Jesus knew He would be crucified soon and would not physically be present with the multitude to heal them. Therefore, Jesus once again emphasized having faith in Him; to everyone who believes in Jesus, all things are possible. You may ask how to have mountain-moving faith. Jesus gave us the Holy Spirit after He left us two thousand years ago. Once you are saved, the Holy Spirit residing in you can help build faith. How do you do that? The Bible says faith comes by hearing and hearing the Word of God (Romans 10:17). Thus, it is required for all Christians to listen to godly man preaching the Word of God. Set apart time daily to listen to at least one sermon. Being around people of faith will help us grow stronger in having confidence in God.

We can build faith, and faith increases little by little. Reading the Word, praying with other believers, and listening to praise and worship songs contribute to building faith. We do not need to feel to have faith. More importantly, we must believe in Jesus, keep our eyes focused on Jesus, and the Lord will complete our faith. Let me inspire you with another scripture on faith. The scripture is Matthew 17:20:

> So Jesus said to them, "Because of your unbelief; for assuredly, I say to you, if you have faith as a mustard seed, you will say to this mountain, 'Move from here to there,' and it will move, and nothing will be impossible for you."

Wow, that is a powerful statement from the Lord Jesus. The Lord said having a tiny little faith can make things happen. The power of God is released when we have true faith, and that faith is in Jesus, and Jesus is in us through the Holy Spirit, which makes faith manifest.

The Power of Love

One new commandment Jesus gave us in the New Testament was to love one another. In John 13:34–35, Jesus said, "A new commandment I give to you, that you love one another; as I have loved you, you also love one another. By this, all will know that you are My disciples if you love one another." This is powerful teaching from the Lord Jesus. You must remember that Jesus was also God in the flesh while He was on earth. He knew what was coming in the future. In Timothy 3:1–3, the scripture says, "But know this, that in the last days perilous times will come: For men will be lovers of themselves, lovers of money, boasters, proud, blasphemers, disobedient to parents, unthankful, unholy, unloving, unforgiving, slanderers, without self-control, brutal, despisers of good." The scripture from Timothy was written by one of the fellow-workers of God. Timothy was a companion to Apostle Paul, who contributed to New Testament writing after Jesus left the earth. Apostle Paul had written thirteen out of twenty-seven books in the New Testament, and Timothy was a co-author for some New Testament books. Apostles Paul and Timothy had written under the guidance of the Holy Spirit, giving them the wisdom to teach and preach the Word of God.

When there is no love or lack of love in the world, it can lead to disunity, disagreement on every level, chaos, hatred, envy, murder, and war. 1 Corinthians 13:4–7 says, "Love suffers long and is kind; love does not envy; love does not parade itself, is not puffed up; does not behave rudely, does not seek its own, is not provoked, thinks no evil; does not rejoice in iniquity, but rejoices in the truth; bears all things, believes all things, hopes all things, endures all things." Love suffers long; in other words, it means love is patient, and the rest of the scripture is self-explanatory. God has a high standard of love.

We, humans, have a pretty narrow mentality about the subject of love. Our love is about two people of the opposite sex loving each other; we also love people we care about, like our parents, children, close relatives, and friends. I don't deny that loving people keep the bond tight, harmonious, and peaceful, making us capable of giving and receiving respect and helping each other generously; thus, love is beautiful. But God loves the unlikable, the enemies, the ugly, and the rejects, and Jesus also loved those who killed Him on the cross. On the day He was hanging on the cross, He said, "Father, forgive them, for they do not know what they do" (Luke 23:34). The Lord forgives those who hurt Him without any partiality; the Lord came for the sinners, and He even loved them more when they repented of their sins. For those who repented of their sins and received Him, He gave them the right to become children of God (John 1:12). Wow, now this is unconditional love.

We humans may forgive people who did us wrong in the past, but it is hard or almost impossible to love them. But God's love surpasses our knowledge and understanding because God is God in His very nature. God loves sinners; He can break the heart of stone into a heart of flesh through the power of His love. In Ezekiel 36:26–27, the Lord said, "I will give you a new heart and put a new spirit within you; I will take the heart of stone out of your flesh and give you a heart of flesh. I will put My Spirit within you and cause you to walk in My statutes, and you will keep My judgments and do them." Wow, only God can do this, and this is called the power of God's love.

God is love (1 John 4:8, 16); it is in His nature. God saves people from going to the lake of fire. God desires all the individuals on this earth to be protected and bring them to a place called heaven. Once you are saved, God keeps no evil records from your past (1 Corinthians 13:5). Upon receiving Jesus into your heart, you are born again; you are a new creature leaving the old and walking into the new life. The Lord will work with you through His Holy Spirit to make you a more loving person. Even if you have difficulty forgiving anyone who has abused, betrayed, cheated, and rejected you in the past, God can transform your mind and change your heart, if you yield to the Holy Spirit. How do you yield to the Holy Spirit? Daily worship and praise God for Who He is, read the Bible, spend time in prayer, talk to God about things that bother you, and be transparent to God. There is no need to hide anything from God; He knows everything, by the way. Give time for God to work with you. Never forsake the gathering with all the other saints in your church, and attend Bible study to help you grow into a more mature Christian.

The Holy Spirit in you is God, and He loves you, and He will make you love those unlovable, just like Jesus. Love is one of the fruits of the Spirit you will see in a Christ believer. Apostle Paul is our example in the Bible, wherein 1 Corinthians 13:1–3 says, "Though I speak with the tongues of men and angels, but have not loved, I have become sounding brass or a clanging cymbal. And though I have the gift of prophecy, understand all mysteries and knowledge, and have all faith so that I could remove mountains, but have not loved, I am nothing. And though I bestow all my goods to feed the poor, and though I give my body to be burned, but have not loved, it profits me nothing." Meanwhile, in 1 Corinthians 13:13, the scripture says, "And now abide faith, hope, love, these three; but the greatest is love."

Love is a powerful substance believers carry in them. Loves drive the believer to pray for the sick, speak a word of hope to others, and have mountain-moving faith in supporting others to overcome almost impossible circumstances. When Jesus saves a person, the person will eventually become less selfish and more people-oriented. Our corrupted minds and narcissistic attitude we had before being born again are gradually cut off when we abide in Jesus and continue to grow in Christian values. When Christ lives in us, we cling to the substance called love, and love is a mighty spear that ultimately will unify people and bring peace to the world, and the world will know we belong to Christ.

I want to share a bit of my salvation story here. When the Lord first touched me, I was in church. An overwhelming heat went through my body, and I sobbed a lot. I felt pure love from God; I almost kneeled from the chair where I was sitting. It is indescribable emotion for me. The cross and crucifixion of Jesus were a symbol of love towards me. I was in that wave of being loved by my Lord, and I wanted Jesus to come into my heart immediately. I wanted the warmness to stay with me as long as possible. Since then, the Lord has captured my heart, and life has taken a 180-degree turn. Wow, what a powerful touch of love from the Lord Jesus. This love is called the power of Jesus's love, which can cause a life to be changed.

The Power of the Blood

The blood reminds me of Jesus dying on the cross, and He shed the blood on that cross. Jesus is not on earth with us, but His Holy Spirit is with us, inside us, and upon us. We see the blood as a powerful symbol with many powerful functions when applied with faith. Jesus, Himself said in Mathew 26:28, "For this is My blood of the new covenant, which is shed for many for the remission of sins." This dialogue occurred when Jesus had the Last Supper with His twelve disciples. The passage meant that blood has the power to redeem us. In Ephesians 1:7, Paul writes, "In Him, we have redemption through His blood, the forgiveness of sins, according to the riches of His grace." Meanwhile, 1 Peter 1:18–19 says, "knowing that you were not redeemed with corruptible things, like silver or gold, from your aimless conduct received by tradition from your fathers, but with the precious blood of Christ, as of a lamb without blemish and without spot."

When we want to be saved, we say the salvation prayer out loud, which includes the blood of Jesus that washes away our sins; therefore, we are forgiven of our past sins, and we are given a new life in Christ Jesus. Just a reminder, the one-time prayer we did when we received Jesus into our hearts does not give us the license to live anyhow we wanted or to be lawless and forget why we were saved. We are to seek Jesus every day after we are redeemed, which is how we can keep ourselves from sinning. Change in our life takes time, and we will face changes throughout our life. The Lord will mold us through failures and successes until we are perfect like Him when we see Him face to face. After the first time of salvation prayer, the Holy Spirit is in us; that is how we have the power to overcome sin by daily seeking the Lord. Salvation is a gift from God that we receive by faith; therefore, we live and walk by faith by holding on to Jesus daily.

The blood brings us close to Jesus. Ephesians 2:13 says, "But now in Christ Jesus, you who once were far off have been brought near by the blood of Christ." You may ask how the blood of Jesus brings us closer. When Jesus died on the cross, the temple's veil was torn in two, which allowed us access to the Holy of Holies (Matthew 27:51). In the Old Testament, there was a holy temple in Jerusalem where only the priest was allowed in to carry out religious activities. A covering or a thick veil in that temple separated the Holy of Holies from the rest of the temple where men dwelt. The separation of the Holy of Holies with a thick veil from other temple parts signifies that men are separated from God due to sin (Hebrews 9:1–9, Isaiah 59:1–2).

In that temple, animal sacrifices were carried out. Only the priest was allowed into the Holy of Holies beyond the heavy curtain covering (Exodus 30:10). The priest sprinkled the sacrificial animal blood with burning incense, which provided temporal removal of the people's sin (Leviticus 16). Since this activity is considered holy, only the priest can carry it out for the people. The spotless lamb is a sin offering for the people of Israel, forgiving their wrongdoings or sins (Leviticus 16:15). The animal sacrifice is a replacement for the sinners, where the animal died in place of the human for their sins. This offering of animal sacrifice is repeated because the forgiveness of sins is only temporary in the Old Covenant.

On the other hand, in the New Covenant, Jesus came as the perfect, blameless, and spotless lamb and died for our sins on the cross. Therefore, there is no need for animal sacrifice anymore. Jesus died once and for all time. Jesus became our mediator between God and humans. There is no need for a High Priest to carry out the sprinkling of the blood with incense burning anymore in the Holy of Holies where the presence of God is present. The moment when the Lord Jesus breath the last breath on the cross, the thick veil covering the Holy of Holies was torn into two, which enabled access to God's presence for all humanity. This is the Heavenly Father's plan for us to have a direct relationship with God and His Son. In Matthew 27:50–51, the Bible informs us, "And Jesus cried out again with a loud voice and yielded up His spirit. Then, behold, the veil of the temple was torn in two from top to bottom, and the earth quaked, and the rocks were split." The shedding of the blood of Jesus on the cross opened the path to God's presence (Hebrews 10:19–20). Wow, the power of the shed blood of Jesus made us have access to God's presence.

The blood of Jesus has the power to protect you

and keep you safe. How do you do this? Of course, by faith, we apply the blood of Jesus over our lives and our surroundings. Recognize that no actual blood is involved, but blood is a symbol used in a believer's life for many powerful reasons. Besides the redemption and cleansing of sin, additionally, in faith, the blood also can protect the believer from demonic spirits or evil spirits. In the Old Testament, Exodus 12:13 says, "Now the blood shall be a sign for you on the houses where you are. And when I see the blood, I will pass over you; and the plague shall not be on you to destroy you when I strike the land of Egypt." The Lord God wanted His people to be released from Egyptian slavery in this passage. God often asked Pharaoh, the ruler of Egypt, to let go of the Israelites who belonged to God. Pharaoh would not let God's people go, keeping them in bondage for a long time. Moses was the chosen man of God to deliver the Israelites from bondage. God sent plague after plague to punish Pharaoh. The final tenth plague killed all the firstborns in Egypt including Pharaoh first born son and finally made Pharaoh to free the Israelites.

Before the final last plague, Lord God instructed His people to sacrifice a lamb and apply the sacrificed lamb's blood on the doorpost to signify that the household belongs to God. This is also a sign of differentiating between the Egyptian family and the Israelites, who believe in God. The Lord God said when the angel of death comes, the evil destroyer will bypass the house with the blood sign, which indicates that the household acknowledges God (Exodus 12:13). Without the blood sign on the doorpost, the angel of death will kill the firstborn in those houses.

The firstborn of Pharaoh was killed that night, and Pharaoh was emotionally disturbed and saddened. He finally let go of the Israelites from Egypt.

The blood used from the sacrificed lamb serves as a sign of protection from the demonic spirit. When Jesus came, He was the flawless lamb that was killed, and the blood that was poured out was holy blood that makes demons tremble and powerless. Jesus became our Passover lamb once and for all, where whoever receives Him as Savior and God has the right to be protected from the wicked demonic spirits. As we see the angel of death bypassing the houses with the blood applied to the doorpost in the Old Testament, today we have the Holy Spirit in us as a seal (2 Corinthians 1:22) and symbolically applying the blood of Jesus (2 Corinthians 1:22), and makes the devil dare not touch the soul of God's people.

Remember that the devil is cunning; his job is to sneak into God's people whenever possible. The devil is a tempter and will try to separate you from God. Therefore, it is a good practice daily to say, "I am applying the blood of Jesus over my life, my possession, my family and home, and my workplace." Remember, the words have power when the Holy Spirit is in you. When you speak it aloud, the devil hears that, making him flee the other way. In Revelation 12:11, the Bible says, "And they overcame him by the blood of the Lamb and by the word of their testimony, and they did not love their lives to the death." It is crucial to understand this passage because it informs us that we can overcome Satan and his works by applying the blood and confessing it through our mouths.

Another reason the blood of Jesus is powerful is its

healing power. How does it heal our body from sickness and infirmities? 1 Corinthians 11:27–30 says, "Therefore whoever eats this bread or drinks this cup of the Lord in an unworthy manner will be guilty of the body and blood of the Lord. But let a man examine himself, so let him eat of the bread and drink of the cup. He who eats and drinks in an unworthy manner eats and drinks judgment to himself, not discerning the Lord's body. For this reason, many are weak and sick among you, and many sleep." This scripture talks about taking Communion, or the last supper.

The Last Supper was the Passover meal Jesus had with His twelve disciples before His crucifixion. In the Old Testament, during the Passover night, the shedding of the blood protected the Israelites from the angel of death, and eating of the flesh of the same roasted sacrificed lamb made none of the Israelites feeble or sick (Psalm 105:37). Of course, the blood has the power to cleanse and provide forgiveness for our sins and ultimately redeem us but never forget it also brings healing to the sick body. You have to remember to do this communion in faith to receive healing through the shed blood of Jesus. In Matthew 8:17, the scripture says, "that it might be fulfilled which Isaiah the prophet spoke, saying: He took our infirmities And bore our sicknesses."

This passage means that the Lord Jesus had taken our infirmities and sickness through His beating and nailing on the cross. Once again, I would remind you to do this in faith to receive healing from your sickness. There are many reasons for being sick, but it is for His glory when the Lord heals you. I wanted to clarify that when you don't get healed, never lose hope; our God is sovereign, and He knows what He is doing. Our part is to have faith in Him and strengthen our faith in Jesus because heaven is waiting. Sickness itself is not a sin, but sinning toward God can cause a person to be sick and die (Micah 6:13).

There is no doubt that the blood of Jesus washes away our sin, and that is a fact, but questioning God why some don't get healed from their bodily sickness, that only God can answer; our job is to have faith in the healing power of God through His shed blood on Calvary. Communion is carried out in churches every Sunday, once a month, or sometimes once every two to three months. I wanted to let you know that communion can be held daily in your home. What you need is a piece of small bread and grape juice. When you take communion, you are reminding yourself of the crucifixion of Jesus two thousand years back, looking forward to His return in the future (1 Corinthians 11:26), and believing in healing in your body. When you do so, say this:

> Thank you, Lord, for dying on the cross for my sins. I am doing this in remembrance that You have died on the cross for my sins, and You have taken away my sicknesses, diseases, and infirmities. Lord, this bread [it can be a piece of bread or biscuit] represents Your broken body on the cross [eat the bread now, then move on to the cup of grape juice].

Lord, this grape juice represents Your blood that was shed on the cross for my sins. I am doing this in remembrance that You have died on the cross for my sins and taken away my sickness, diseases, and infirmities. Thank You, Lord [drink the juice].

This is my way of taking communion; I know it sounds redundant with the prayer, but I advise you to ask your pastor or any godly person in the church to teach you how to take communion at home. I do it almost daily after my prayer. I learned that home communion prayer from a pastor.

I wanted to recap here on the power of the blood of Jesus. As a believer, we must know that the blood of Jesus has the power to cleanse, forgive, redeem our sins, and protect us from demonic or evil spirits. The blood applied in faith has the capacity to heal our bodies from sickness and infirmities. Oh, how precious is the blood the Lord Jesus shed on the cross. He did it for you and me, so we can live a powerful life in Jesus via His blood.

The Power of the Gifts

As believers of Christ, we must be continually filled with the power of the Holy Spirit daily. Why do we need daily infilling of the power of the Holy Spirit? We seek God daily and ask for the fresh infilling of the Holy Spirit to empower us to live the Christian life. When we are continually filled, the fullness of the Spirit will flow out from us and touch the lives of others. You know we received the Holy Spirit when we received Jesus for the first time in our hearts. But continually asking the Lord to fill us afresh with His power daily makes us so full of the Spirit that it enables us to give it away as a blessing to people around us. Imagine a cup filled to the top that overflows and drips down; that is how the overflow of Spirit works.

Why am I touching on the infilling and overflow of the Spirit? If you know what Jesus carries with Him, you know that the same Spirit in you will manifest from you and be a blessing to the surrounding people. It is a fact that Jesus heals broken hearts and sickness; He knows the past and future of a person; He is a miracle worker, He is the greatest Teacher of all times, and above all, He is God. Therefore, when you are continually filled with the

Spirit of Jesus in you, also called the Holy Spirit power, you may see the power of the Spirit work the same from you. When you pray for the sick, they get healed; when you teach the Word of God to others, it seems to be powerful teaching and touches the lives of unbelievers and believers; some of us may even have the gift of prophecies and see things happen precisely in the future.

To go into more detail, these are the overflows of the Spirit. Jesus gives you the gifts to edify and unify the church for the glory of God. These are not ordinary gifts; they are called spiritual gifts from the Heavenly Father. Our heavenly Father empowers us with these spiritual gifts to accomplish His work on earth. Yes, the church is the first place where the gifts are employed, and in addition, they are given to carry out the mission on earth that God has, and He gives explicitly different gifts to each one of us.

All of these gifts are from one source from our Heavenly Father so we can be a witness to Christ. In the church, we practice using it to edify, comfort, and uplift each other with love. Meanwhile, these signs and wonders in the mission field confirm that God is here on earth among us and to draw all men to Jesus for salvation. I want to show you the different gifts God can give us. In Ephesians 4:11–13, the scripture says, "And He gave some to be apostles, some prophets, some evangelists, and some pastors and teachers, for the equipping of the saints for the work of ministry, for the edifying of the body of Christ, till we all come to the unity of the faith and the knowledge of the Son of God, to a perfect man, to the measure of the stature of the fullness of Christ." In this passage, these gifts are called "ministry" gifts. Ministry means serving God or carrying out the spiritual work He called you to do on this earth.

Meanwhile, in 1 Corinthians 12:7–10, the Bible mentions, "But the manifestation of the Spirit is given to each one for the profit of all: for to one is given the word of wisdom through the Spirit, to another the word of knowledge through the same Spirit, to another faith by the same Spirit, to another gift of healings, the working of miracles, to another prophecy, to another discerning of spirits, to other different kinds of tongues, and finally the interpretation of tongues." These are called the manifestation gifts. The manifestation gifts are meant to benefit others and your personal growth as a Christian. For example, we can ask for a word of wisdom regarding a specific situation we are facing or ask for discernment of Spirit to discern error from the truth; in 1 John 4:1, Saint John the Apostle said, "Beloved, do not believe every spirit, but test the spirits, whether they are of God; because many false prophets have gone out into the world." These gifts enable you to witness the living God's power and presence.

Additionally, in Romans 12:6–8, we are made aware of the scripture informing us that "Having then gifts differing according to the grace that is given to us, let us use them: if prophecy, let us prophesy in proportion to our faith; or ministry, let us use it in our ministering; he who teaches, in teaching; he who exhorts, in exhortation; he who gives, with liberality; he who leads, with diligence; he who shows mercy, with cheerfulness." These are called motivational gifts from God.

At times, we tend to have all the gifts mentioned; nevertheless, God can anoint you with one or two or even three specific gifts. The particular gifts are given to enlighten and build the body of the church, accomplish the mission on this earth, and ultimately bring glory to His name. Now, why does the Lord graciously anoint you? First, let me define anointing, so we can understand it. Anointing is a supernatural power God graciously gives to His sons and daughters to be authentic witnesses for Christ. Jesus's heart is for the lost world, and He wants to draw all men to Him, so no one goes to the eternal lake of fire. He loves all humans and died for all of us to give life more abundantly and bring you to the eternal place called heaven when we leave this earth.

Humans are skeptical; they don't believe you unless they see miracles or supernatural events. Therefore, supernatural power is used as evidence that there is a living God in this universe, and He wants to save our souls from perishing in hell (John 3:16). When supernatural things happen, it is also evidence to the unbeliever (and, surprisingly, to many believers too) that God's Spirit lives in a human body to empower humans to do the things only God can do through them. All believers are called to be a witness to Christ. In Acts 1:8, the Bible says, "But you shall receive power when the Holy Spirit has come upon you, and you shall be witnesses to Me in Jerusalem, and all Judea and Samaria, and to the end of the earth." That verse was Jesus talking to His disciples and followers.

I hope you will study each spiritual gift in-depth, and I want you to ask God what specific gift He has for you, so you may discover that anointing in your life to be fruitful for the Kingdom of God. Understand me; you did have the power of the Holy Spirit in you when you were born again for the first time. However, God does have a special calling for every person He saves, and He anoints you with that specific spiritual gift for the benefit of others. Remember, the scripture in Jeremiah 1:5; the Bible says, "Before I formed you in the womb I knew you; Before you were born I sanctified you; I ordained you a prophet to the nations." In that verse from the Old Testament, God was telling Jeremiah that He ordained Jeremiah as the prophet to the nations; likewise, God knew us before He formed us in our mother's womb, and He has a special calling for us as well. Therefore, seek God fervently, know your purpose on this earth, and accomplish it with the supernatural power God anoints you with.

Before I end this chapter, I want you to realize that whatever Jesus has in Him, you have it too. The difference is that Jesus was 100 percent God and 100 percent human while walking on this earth. On the other hand, we are human beings 100 percent; however, we have the nature of God in us when the Holy Spirit resides in us. The Holy Spirit is the Spirit of Jesus, which empowers us to live the Christian life. At the same time, Jesus anoints you with a unique power gift, elevating you further as a powerful human to finish strong in your faith and attract all men to Jesus through that special anointing God put in you.

The Power against Evil Spirits

On this earth, there is light and darkness. The Spirit of God is in us, and evil spirits are around us. How do I know the demonic Spirit surrounds us? Revelation 12:9 states, "So the great dragon was cast out, that serpent of old, called the Devil and Satan, who deceives the whole world; he was cast to the earth, and his angels were cast out with him." As long as we are on this earth, there will be a constant battle between the people of God and Satan. This battle is called spiritual warfare. Spiritual warfare is fighting against unseen evil spirits or demonic spirits. When we are saved and born again, we belong to the Kingdom of God; the opposition to God's Kingdom is Satan's kingdom.

Satan dislikes God's people because Satan wants to be like God or be equal with God (Isaiah 14:12–15). But God remains God, and no one is equal to Him; therefore, Satan hates God and His people. What is the job of Satan, then? His job is to constantly disturb the believers of Christ; according to 1 Peter 5:8, "Be sober, be vigilant; because your adversary the devil walks about like a roaring lion, seeking whom he may devour." Meanwhile, in John 10:10, the scriptures state, "The thief does not come except to steal and to kill, and to destroy." Both scriptures say the devil has his plan to damage the life of God's people; why is that so? Because we are human and not God, Satan is sneaky, like the serpent in the Garden of Eden, and He knows how to manipulate our thoughts and emotions. When we fall into the hand of Satan, then Satan wins because he is victorious in separating humans from God.

However, the good news is, Jesus defeated Satan. Satan was cast out from God's dwelling place. God's dwelling place is in heaven, and Satan is no longer up there; he will be cast into the lake of fire forever; meanwhile, demonic spirits are also hovering over the air to devour the believers in Christ. But Christ believers have the Holy Spirit in them. We are the temple of God. Our body is the dwelling place of God (1 Corinthians 6:19). What does this mean? It means the devil does not have a place in a believer's body or life. He is a defeated being in the hands of God and the life of Christians.

Wow, that is a powerful life to live on earth. Jesus overcame the kingdom of darkness on the cross. The scripture from Colossians 1:13–15 is proof we are delivered from the evil one. The scripture states, "He has delivered us from the power of darkness and conveyed us into the kingdom of the Son of His love, in whom we have redemption through His blood, the forgiveness of sins."

Many Christians are ignorant about the power they have against evil spirits. Many Christians today are living a defeated life. How can this happen? First, many of us give place to Satan. We listen to Satan's voice, or maybe we don't even recognize it when Satan is whispering to us, like what happened to Eve in the Garden of Eden. Second, we are drawn into what is happening in the world around us, such as the bad news on the television, the rumors or gossip people are spreading, the COVID-19 pandemic, the unpredictable weather, and many more. Third, it is our fault for being inconsistent with our walk with God; we are more concerned about the current difficulty or stressful moment we are going through. Fourth is the worst; some don't even know we have a real enemy, the devil. Ephesians 6:12 says, "For we do not wrestle against flesh and blood, but principalities, against powers, against the rulers of the darkness of this age, against spiritual hosts of wickedness in the heavenly places."

Let's see how the power of Jesus can work in our lives to live a victorious life on the earth. In John 10:27, Lord Jesus said, "My sheep hear My voice, and I know them, and they follow Me." Do we know the Lord's voice? One thing is for sure, in my personal experience, the Lord speaks in a still, small voice (1 Kings 19:12). However, there are many other ways God can talk to us. He can speak through the scriptures or through a man of God like prophets and through God's people, and also through the preaching of the Word of God by the pastors in the church. Constantly listening to the Word of God, either on television or radio, or even listening to uncorrupted worship songs, will push away the voice of others, especially Satan. When we are acquainted with the Word of God, it is pretty easy to differentiate between God's voice and the devil's.

One must learn to shut the world's noise by hearing God's voice. How do we do that? From the moment we wake up in the morning until we go to bed at night, our minds should focus on Jesus. In the morning, make it a habit to thank God, and then have a dedicated quiet time with God. Quiet time means you are praying, worshipping, reading, and meditating upon the Word of God. If only we could give our very first hour of the day to God, I believe the world's chaos would not affect us that much. Now, why is that so? That is because as we learn and grow in the Word of God, we learn to put our trust in Jesus. We see and think like Jesus.

Let me share what Apostle Paul said about fighting spiritual warfare or, more specifically, how to fight the devil's wiles. The scripture is from Ephesians 6:13–17: "Therefore take up the whole armor of God, that you may be able to withstand in the evil day, and having done all, to stand. Stand therefore, having girded your waist with truth, having put on the breastplate of righteousness, and having shod your feet with the preparation of the Gospel of peace; above all, taking the shield of faith with which you will be able to quench all the fiery darts of the wicked one. And take the helmet of salvation, and the sword of the Spirit, which is the word of God."

The COVID-19 pandemic was a challenging time for many of us. If we allow the pandemic to take over our thoughts and emotions, we will end up in depression. When we know what God says about provision, we will learn to be patient and depend on God for all our needs, despite what's happening to the world. In Philippians 4:19, Apostle Paul said, "And my God shall supply all your need according to His riches in glory by Christ Jesus." I want to put down here what Jesus was teaching about provision. The scripture is from Matthew 6:25–34:

"Therefore I say to you, do not worry about your life, what you will eat or drink; nor about your body, what you will put on. Isn't life more than food and the body more than clothing? Look at the birds of the air, for they neither sow nor reap nor gather into barns; yet your heavenly Father feeds them. Are you not of more value than they? Which of you, by worrying, can add one cubit to his stature? "So why do you worry about clothing? Consider the lilies of the field, how they grow: they neither toil nor spin, and yet I say to you that even Solomon in all his glory was not arrayed like one of these. Now, if God so clothes the grass of the field, which today is, and tomorrow is thrown into the oven, will He not much more clothe you, O you of little faith? "Therefore do not worry, saying, 'What shall we eat?' or 'What shall we drink?' or 'What shall we wear?' For after all these things, the Gentiles seek. For your heavenly Father knows that you need all these things. But seek first the Kingdom of God and His righteousness, and all these things shall be added to you. Therefore, do not worry about tomorrow, for tomorrow will worry about its things. Sufficient for the day is its trouble."

Wow, Jesus knew our hearts very well that we would fall into emotional distress due to financial issues. Jesus knew there would be times of hardship and also glorious moments to enjoy with wealth in this lifetime. Now, why am I sharing these scriptures? Because in challenging times, the devil will take advantage of God's people, and many fall into the devil's lie or trap due to the chaotic circumstances. Devil is cunning and manipulative in many ways, but we will defeat that evil when we stay in God's presence, accompanied by God's Word. The battle is factual, and every Christian should not give an inch of space for the demonic to enter.

Remember, ultimately, victory belongs to God's people because of what Jesus did on the cross. Our responsibility is to remind ourselves daily, spend the first hour with God, read the scripture, listen to godly sermons, worship, and even fast for a short period. Do not neglect attending church on Sunday, worship God with all the other saints, and pray for one another. Be consistent; then, you will see the power of Jesus working in your life to defeat every evil attempt from the devil. I am very sure we are victorious because according to Matthew 28:18, "And Jesus came and spoke to them, saying, 'All authority has been given to Me in heaven and on earth.'" Knowing that we belong to Jesus, we can call upon Jesus, which makes the devil powerless and ultimately has no access or authority over us (Luke 10:17). Wow, what a powerful life in the hands of our Almighty God.

The Power of the Invisible God

Colossians 1:15 says, "He is the image of the invisible God, the firstborn over all creation." Two thousand years ago, Jesus walked on earth as a physically living being, seen as a human. Nevertheless, He is also God and was called God in the flesh. Jesus was conceived through the power of the Holy Spirit in Virgin Mary's womb, and He was born in a typical fashion, like any other child. I want to remind you of the ultimate purpose of why Jesus as a human baby was sent down to this earth by the Heavenly Father.

Jesus was born to fulfill the Heavenly Father's will to redeem us, model godly living, and give us eternal life. One of the Heavenly Father's intentions was for Jesus to be crucified on the cross on our behalf, as an atonement for sin. In 2 Corinthians 5:21, the scripture says, "For He made Him who knew no sin to be sin for us, that we might become the righteousness of God in Him." Yes, our sins are forgiven by believing and accepting Jesus as our Savior and Lord, and we have a place in heaven once we die, but that is not the end. Now we must live daily as a Christ-follower; we are not to be conformed to this world but to be transformed by renewing the mind

(Romans 12:2). We are to have the mind of Christ (1 Corinthians 2:16). Finally, we are to be perfect like our Almighty God in our conduct and in our mind when we meet Him face to face in heaven.

I urge you to read the entire book of John in the Bible. The Gospel of John confirms to us in a deep, profound, heart-touching way that Jesus is the Son of God. Every word Jesus spoke in that Gospel is life and Spirit, which will convict you that Jesus is the Christ. In the same scripture, Jesus informs us He will send us the Holy Spirit so we are not left orphans after His crucifixion. In John 16:7, the Lord said, "Nevertheless I tell you the truth. It is to your advantage that I go away; for if I do not go away, the Helper will not come to you; but if I depart, I will send Him to you."

Meanwhile, in John 15:26–27, Jesus said, "I will send you the Helper from the Father. The Helper is the Spirit of truth who comes from the Father. When he comes, he will tell me about myself. And you will tell people about me too because you have been with me from the beginning." Let me give you another scripture, where Jesus said, "And I will pray for the Father. He will give you another Helper, that He may abide with you forever" (John 14:16). Now, why am I telling you all this? I want to establish you in the knowledge of God that God is Spirit (John 4:24) and Spirit is invisible. Why is this important? Because Jesus left us two thousand years ago, but we have the Holy Spirit here on earth now. Now, what is Holy Spirit? Holy Spirit is not just a person but a divine person; He is holy and a member of the Godhead. Our God is three in one: God the Father, Son, and Holy Spirit. Therefore, Holy Spirit is God.

In my journey in searching for God, I wanted to see God face to face; only then would I believe there was a God. When my search ended at the feet of Jesus, I did not see Jesus face to face, but there was something I felt was special. That feeling was love, comfort, and security. Then I learned it was the presence of God; I don't see Him, but I can sense Him. I met Jesus in a church and got saved that very first time in church. Since then, I have been in love with Jesus, Who is everything in my life. Coming from a different faith background, I am convinced that Jesus is God, and He is the way, the life, and the truth, and nobody goes to the Father except through Jesus (John 14:6).

Jesus said in John 14:20, "If you had known Me, you would have known My Father also; and from now on you know Him and have seen Him." In conclusion, God the Father looks like you and me. What separates us from the unbelievers is the Holy Spirit in us. The Holy Spirit sealed us as a sign that we belong to Jesus. In Ephesians 1:13–14, the scripture says, "In Him, you also trusted, after you heard the word of truth, the Gospel of your salvation; in whom also, having believed, you were sealed with the Holy Spirit of promise, who is the guarantee of our inheritance until the redemption of the purchased possession, to the praise of His glory."

I have been writing at quite a length about the power of the invisible God. That is because I wanted you to know that our God is invisible. He is in Spirit form, but we know He looks like you and me, if He has a physical body. As Christians, we must learn to live with the invisible God. God is in us, with us, and upon us. In my walk with

God, I have tangibly sensed the presence of God. At times during the worship service in the church and personal worship at home, I get the heat going through my body, sometimes pulsation throughout the body, sometimes a cool breeze. This is called the tangible presence of God. God loves to be worshiped and touches you uniquely, so you can feel He is there sensibly.

The invisible God that lives in us, who is called the Holy Spirit, has the power to transform our lives, protect us, provide for us, heal our broken hearts and our ill body, cast out demonic spirits, and endure the hardship of life, and also the supernatural power to help others via the spiritual gifts that have been given to us. Let's see the bigger picture of God; He is the creator of heaven and earth (Genesis 1:1). Let me give you more from the book of Genesis to show you who God is. The below passage is from Genesis 1:26–31:

> Then God said, "Let Us make man in Our image, according to Our likeness; let them have dominion over the fish of the sea, over the birds of the air, and the cattle, over all the earth and over every creeping thing that creeps on the earth." So God created man in His image; in the image of God, He created him; male and female, He created them. Then God blessed them, saying to them, "Be fruitful and multiply; fill the earth and subdue it; have dominion over the fish of the sea, the birds of the air, and every living thing that moves on the earth."

And God said, "See, I have given you every herb that yields seed which is on the face of all the earth, and every tree whose fruit yields seed; to you, it shall be for food. Also, to every beast of the earth, to every bird of the air, and to everything that creeps on the earth, in which there is life, I have given every green herb for food,"; and it was so. Then God saw everything that He had made, and indeed it was perfect. So the evening and the morning were the sixth days.

Well, you can see that God is a creator. He is a powerful creator; apart from Him, the earth is non-existence. Of course, we were not there to see with our eyes God created it, but we know He did it by speaking it out. We Christians must know and believe that God is Spirit, and He is all-powerful, all-knowing, and all-present. In other words, He is omnipotent, omniscient, and omnipresent. Right now, Jesus is not with us, but His Holy Spirit is, and you cannot see the Holy Spirit with your eyes. Many scriptures in the Bible teach us to have faith and believe without seeing it with our naked eyes. In John 20:29, Jesus said, "Thomas, because you have seen Me, you have believed. Blessed are those who have not seen and yet have believed." I also want to clarify that God's omnipresence differs from God's manifest presence. Omnipresence means God is with us every time and everywhere. You will not feel Him or sense Him, but He is there 24/7 with you.

On the other hand, the manifest presence of God is when you are aware He is there with you, and it is clear that God is doing something to show you His presence. What I mean is, you will see the works of God, and you will know it is God's doing to show us He is with us. Our God is experiential. There are many examples of the manifestation of the presence of God in the Old Testament and the New Testament. In the Old Testament, a good example is Exodus 3:1–6, where the Lord spoke to Moses:

> Now Moses was tending the flock of Jethro his father-in-law, the priest of Midian. And he led the flock to the back of the desert and came to Horeb, the mountain of God. And the Angel of the Lord appeared to him in a flame of fire from the midst of a bush. So he looked; behold, the bush was burning with fire, but the bush was not consumed. Then Moses said, "I will now turn aside and see this great sight, why the bush does not burn." So when the Lord saw that he turned aside to look, God called to him from the midst of the bush and said, "Moses, Moses!" And he said, "Here I am." Then He said, "Do not draw near this place. Take your sandals off your feet, for where you stand is holy ground." Moreover, He said, "I am the God of your father—the God of Abraham, the

God of Isaac, and the God of Jacob." And
Moses hid his face, for he was afraid to
look upon God.

That is an example of the manifest presence of God.
God appeared to Moses in the burning bush, but the fire
did not consume the bush. Instead, God called and spoke
to Moses from that burning bush and instructed him to
deliver the Israelites from the hand of the Egyptians. I
want you to see that God makes His presence known to
Moses without physically showing His face and body.
God had been present with Moses all this while, but at
the burning bush, He revealed Himself clearly by giving
Moses the signs like the burning bush and His voice.

Let me give you another example of the manifested
presence of God in the Old Testament. This can be found
in Genesis 18:1, which says, "Then the Lord appeared to
him by the terebinth trees of Mamre, as he was sitting
in the tent door in the heat of the day." In this scripture,
the Lord appeared to Abraham to deliver a message.
The Lord appeared in a human form. Let me put down
the rest of the scripture for you to read and be clear on
the manifested presence of God that was made aware to
Abraham. This scripture is from Genesis 18:2–10:

So he lifted his eyes and looked, and
behold, three men were standing by him;
and when he saw them, he ran from the
tent door to meet them, bowed himself
to the ground, and said, "My Lord, if I
have now found favor in Your sight, do

not pass on by Your servant. Please let a little water be brought, wash your feet, and rest yourselves under the tree. And I will bring a morsel of bread that you may refresh your hearts. After that, you may pass by since you have come to your servant." They said, "Do as you have said." So Abraham hurried into the tent to Sarah and said, "Quickly, make ready three measures of fine meal; knead it and make cakes." And Abraham ran to the herd, took a tender and good calf, gave it to a young man, and hastened to prepare it. So he took butter, milk, and the calf he had designed and set it before them, and he stood by them under the tree as they ate. Then they said to him, "Where is Sarah, your wife?" So he said, "Here, in the tent." And He said, "I will certainly return to you according to the time of life, and behold, Sarah, your wife shall have a son."

I wanted you to know that God can manifest Himself in an image of a human, and that is in the Old Testament. Now, I want you to see the examples of God's manifested presence in the New Testament. In Acts 2:2–4, the scripture says, "And suddenly there came a sound from heaven, as of a mighty rushing wind, and it filled the whole house where they were sitting. Then there appeared divided tongues, as of fire, and one sat upon each of them. And they were all filled with the Holy Spirit and began to speak with other tongues, as the Spirit gave them utterance." By the way, this event happened after Jesus left the earth. I want you to know that God showed His presence with a sound that came down from heaven with a strong wind and touched each one of the disciples like fire and filled them with the Holy Spirit, and gave them utterance to speak with others' tongues. In this scripture, speaking in tongues means speaking in different languages (foreign languages). The disciple spoke in languages they did not know, but those unbelievers who speak other languages would hear the finished work of Christ on the cross and be saved. The purpose of the gift of speaking in tongues, specifically in this context or scripture, is to spread the Gospel of Christ, enlighten others, and bring them to salvation. It is to win the loss to Christ. It is a gift from God, and some people have this type of gift today.

I don't want you to get confused with speaking in the spirit, also called speaking in tongues. For example, in 1 Corinthians 14:2, Apostle Paul said, "For he who speaks in a tongue does not speak to men but God, for no one understands him; however, in the spirit, he speaks mysteries." The point here is, I want you to see the manifested presence of God, where you are aware that God is there and the works He performs.

Let me give you another example of the manifested presence of God from the New Testament. In Acts 22:6–8, the scripture says, "Now it happened, as I journeyed and came near Damascus at about noon, suddenly a great light from heaven shone around me. And I fell to the ground and heard a voice saying, 'Saul, Saul, why are you persecuting Me?' So I answered, 'Who are You, Lord?' And He said, 'I am Jesus of Nazareth, whom you are persecuting.'"

I want you to see that light and a sound came from above. Saul immediately called that light Lord; he knew it was God. Then Jesus spoke to Saul. Saul got converted directly, his name was changed to Paul, and he was an influential apostle of Christ who preached and performed miracles. Many were restored, and the Gospel spread further in many world regions. The point here is, you don't see Jesus, though He manifested differently for Apostle Paul.

Have you ever experienced the manifested presence of God in your walk with Jesus? Many people are familiar with the name Holy Ghost from the Bible. What they have in their mind is a ghost. People talk more about ghosts than God. It seems like ghost is more interesting than the invisibility of our God Jesus. Many see ghost movies or play with Ouija boards or black magic, witchcraft, and spell casting, and some adore angelic angels to bring them good luck, which is all the spirit of divinity. If you have ever done this or still play with it, you are in danger because it will destroy your life. I urge you to repent from sin, give your life back to Christ, and invite the Holy Spirit back into your life.

How do you keep yourself focused on the Holy Spirit? First, acknowledge His presence, and talk to Him because the Holy Spirit is a Person, and He is God. Read the Bible and meditate upon the Word of God, worship Him, put on songs of adoration about Jesus, pray and fellowship with people from the church, and listen to godly men preaching the Word of God. I also urge you to speak to your pastor if you are unsure whether you are still involved or had been involved in the occult. Some baby Christians can be carried away by the occult because they may have encountered or experienced supernatural power, but it is counterfeit power that is not from Jesus. This matter is serious and must be cut off immediately because it is demonic, and you have to rededicate your life to Jesus. The counterfeit spirit is also invisible, which enables you to see the power, which is why baby Christians may innocently fall into that influence.

How do you know you are with the Holy Spirit and the manifested presence of God is from Jesus? You will know it when it is aligned with the Word of God. That is why reading the Bible and listening to the Word of God daily is crucial in Christian life. Once you are familiar with the Word of God, keeping your thoughts on God, spending private time in prayer, listening to worship songs, attending church and Bible study will keep you in step with God, and you will become familiar with the Holy Spirit. You can easily differentiate between the Holy Spirit and the spirit of divination or a demonic spirit. The Lord said in John 10:27, "My sheep hear My voice, and I know them, and they follow Me." Do you recognize Jesus's voice? Therefore, start doing what I mentioned earlier; our God is loving and faithful, never leaves nor forsakes you, and created you in His image. He wants to have a relationship with you, and trust me, you will walk in step with Jesus, and you will experience the manifested presence of the invisible God in your life.

Wow, what a powerful life we have as Christians, and through this, we can impact the people around us and the world. Why? Because signs and wonder follow those who believe in Jesus.

Let me finish this chapter with this verse from Mark 16:17–18: "And these signs will follow those who believe: In My name, they will cast out demons; they will speak with new tongues; they will take up serpents; and if they drink anything deadly, it will by no means hurt them; they will lay hands on the sick, and they will recover."

The Power of Resurrection

Romans 8:11 says, "But if the Spirit of Him who raised Jesus from the dead dwells in you, He who raised Christ from the dead will also give life to your mortal bodies through His Spirit who dwells in you." It is not the end when we Christians die. Once we finish our course on earth or our mission on earth completes, our spirit goes to be with our Lord Jesus immediately. In Ecclesiastes 12:7, the Bible says, "Then the dust will return to the earth as it was, And the spirit will return to God who gave it." *Dust* in that verse means the human body. We, humans, are made from the dust of the ground by our Heavenly Father. The first man, Adam, was created by God, which can be found in Genesis 2:7, which says, "And the Lord God formed man of the dust of the ground, and breathed into his nostrils the breath of life; man became a living being."

God did not stop at that. He went on to create helper for the man. The helper is called the woman. Lord God made a woman from the rib of Adam. In Genesis 2:18, the Bible says, "And the Lord God said, "It is not good that man should be alone; I will make him a helper comparable to him." And this is how God created woman; Genesis 2:21–23 says

> And the Lord God caused a deep sleep to fall on Adam, and he slept, and He took one of his ribs and closed up the flesh in its place. Then the rib which the Lord God had taken from man He made into a woman, and He brought her to the man. And Adam said: "This is now bone of my bones And flesh of my flesh; She shall be called Woman because she was taken out of Man."

This portion of scripture is essential because it informs us how humanity was created. God created humans and breathed the breath of life to make us living beings. We know He is the creator of humans and put the spirit of life in us. Therefore, He is also responsible for taking our Spirit up to heaven when we die, and the body or the dust will return to the earth as it was (Ecclesiastes 12:7). As a born again, our spirit goes up to God immediately once we die. The body on earth will be disintegrated or crushed.

The body or the dust left behind will be resurrected on the day of rapture. The soul or the spirit that went up to be with Jesus will be joined together with the dead body from the earth. We will have a gloried body, like Jesus's resurrected body (1 John 3:2, Philippians 3:21). Apostle Paul said, "Behold, I tell you a mystery: We shall not all sleep, but we shall all be changed—in a moment, in the twinkling of an eye, at the last trumpet. The trumpet will sound, the dead will be raised incorruptible, and we shall be changed" (1 Corinthians 15:51–52). This scripture tells us about the rapture that will happen in a split-second.

We do not know the day or time of the rapture because it is a secret God keeps. But God gave the signs of the end of the age or the end of times before the rapture takes place. These signs were mentioned in the Bible where Jesus was teaching His disciples and can be read from Matthew 24:3–14:

> Now, as He sat on the Mount of Olives, the disciples came to Him privately, saying, "Tell us, when will these things be? And what will be the sign of Your coming, and the end of the age?"

> And Jesus answered them: "Take heed that no one deceives you. Many will come in My name, saying, 'I am the Christ,' and deceive many. And you will hear of wars and rumors of wars. See that you are not troubled, for all these things must pass, but the end is not yet. For nation will rise against nation and kingdom against kingdom. And there will be famines, pestilences, and earthquakes in various places. All these are the beginning of sorrows. Then they will deliver you up to tribulation and kill you, and all nations will hate you for My name's sake. And

then many will be offended, will betray one another, and will hate one another. Then many false prophets will arise and deceive many. And because lawlessness will abound, the love of many will grow cold. But he who endures to the end shall be saved. And this gospel of the kingdom will be preached in all the world as a witness to all the nations, and then the end will come."

In 1 Thessalonians 4:13–18 from the New Testament, the scripture elaborates more on how the dead will meet Jesus on the day of rapture. This teaching is from Apostle Paul, who said, "But I do not want you to be ignorant, brethren, concerning those who have fallen asleep, lest you sorrow as others who have no hope. For if we believe that Jesus died and rose again, even so, God will bring with Him those who sleep in Jesus. For this, we say to you by the word of the Lord that we who are alive and remain until the coming of the Lord will by no means precede those who are asleep. For the Lord, Himself will descend from heaven with a shout, the voice of an archangel, and the trumpet of God. And the dead in Christ will rise first. Then we who remain alive shall be caught up with them in the clouds to meet the Lord in the air. And thus, we shall always be with the Lord. Therefore, comfort one another with these words."

The resurrection of the body and reunion with the spirit is a powerful act of God, and this will happen only to those who are born again or by other means; they died in Jesus. The word "fallen asleep" or "sleep" in this scripture from 1 Thessalonians means died. But to those Christians still alive during the rapture, the scripture says that those people will be brought up to the sky and meet up with Jesus in the air; at that time, we will be conformed to the image of Jesus (1 Thessalonians 4:17, Romans 8:29).

Meanwhile, in John 5:25–29, Lord Jesus said, "Most assuredly, I say to you, the hour is coming, and now is, when the dead will hear the voice of the Son of God; and those who hear will live. As the Father has life in Himself, He has granted the Son to have life in Himself and has given Him authority to execute judgment because He is the Son of Man. Do not marvel at this; for the hour is coming in which all who are in the graves will hear His voice and come forth—those who have done good, to the resurrection of life, and those who have done evil, to the resurrection of condemnation." Wow, this scripture here is clear about what will happen to those who followed and stayed faithful to Jesus and those who lived wickedly, despite knowing Jesus but rejecting to the call to be saved.

As a believer of Christ, we must be ready for any time for the rapture to take place. Jesus said in Matthew 24:36–44, "But of that day and hour no one knows, not even the angels of heaven, but My Father only. But as Noah's days were, so will the coming of the Son of Man be. For as in the days before the flood, they were eating and drinking, marrying and giving in marriage, until the day that Noah entered the ark, and did not know until the flood came and took them all away, so also will the coming of the Son of Man be. Then two men will be in the field: one will be taken, and the other left. Two women will grind at the mill: one will be taken, and the other left. Watch therefore, for you do not know what hour your Lord is coming. But know that if the master of the house had known what hour the thief would come, he would have watched and not allowed his house to be broken into. Therefore, be ready, for the Son of Man is coming at an hour you do not expect."

The born-again Christian or those who are faithful in the body of Christ will not be on this earth when the rapture takes place and after the rapture. We will be with Jesus, face to face with Him. At this time, we will be judged for everything we have done as believers in Christ Jesus. We will be rewarded according to our work. This is also called the first judgment of God to His people. In 1 Corinthians 3:8, the Bible states, "Now he who plants and he who waters are one, and each one will receive his reward according to his labor." In Revelation 2:12, the scripture says, "And behold, I am coming quickly, and My reward is with Me, to give to every one according to his work."

The Lord had prepared crowns for His beloved according to the calling we have embraced gracefully and completed it to the end. In 1 Peter 5:4, the Bible informs us, "And when the Chief Shepherd appears, you will receive the crown of glory that does not fade away." Meanwhile, in 1 Corinthians 9:25, Apostle Paul said, "And everyone who competes for the prize is temperate in all things. Now they do it to obtain a perishable crown, but we for an imperishable crown." Additionally, in 2 Timothy 4:8, the Bible says, "Finally, there is laid up for me the crown of righteousness, which the Lord, the righteous Judge, will give to me on that Day, and not to me only but also to all who have loved His appearing."

After the saints are taken or saved by Jesus, the seven-year tribulation begins on earth (Daniel 9:24–27). The tribulation times are also known as the day of the Lord (Isaiah 2:12, 1 Thessalonians 5:2). During this tribulation period, there will be great suffering and persecution. The Antichrist will conquer the world, horrible things like killing, rape, and robbery, the world will be in darkness, and water supplies will be poisoned; it is a time of great distress and nightmares (Zephaniah 1:15, Jeremiah 30:7, Revelation 8:10–11). But remember, the redeemed faithful servant of God will not be on this earth at that time (Revelation 3:10). The church or the body of Christ is saved from the wrath of God (1 Thessalonians 5:9).

After seven years of tribulation, the Lord will come to earth to stop the evil called the "second coming of Jesus" (Jude 1:14–15, Matthew 24:27–31). Let me put here Matthew 24:27–31:

> As the lightning comes from the east and flashes to the west, so will the coming of the Son of Man. For wherever the carcass is, there the eagles will be gathered together. Immediately after the tribulation of those days, the sun will be darkened, and the moon will not give its light; the stars will fall from heaven, and the powers of the heavens will be shaken. Then the sign of the Son of Man will

appear in heaven, and then all the tribes of the earth will mourn, and they will see the Son of Man coming on the clouds of heaven with power and great glory. And He will send His angels with a great trumpet sound, and they will gather His elect from the four winds, from one end of heaven to the other.

In Acts 1:10–11, there was an event where Jesus was taken up to heaven after His resurrection in the presence of the eleven apostles. This is what the Bible wrote: "And while they looked steadfastly toward heaven as He went up, behold, two men stood by them in white apparel, who also said, 'Men of Galilee, why do you stand gazing up into heaven? This same Jesus, who was taken up from you into heaven, will so come in like manner as you saw Him go into heaven.'"

The above is the future coming event on this earth. The event is not yet happened; we as Christians have to hold on to these Bible prophecies. Why? Can the Bible be trusted? First, the Bible is the infallible Word of God (2 Timothy 3:16). Second, every prophecy with the first coming of Jesus has been fulfilled: the birth of Jesus (Isaiah 7:14, Isaiah 9:6), the crucifixion (Isaiah 50:6, Zechariah 12:10), and the resurrection (Isaiah 25:8). The prophecies are in the Old Testament, and every one of them came true in the New Testament. The entire Bible points to Jesus; the coming of the Messiah was prophesied in the Old Testament and fulfilled in the New Testament.

In the second coming of Jesus, He will descend

to Mount Olives in Israel (Zechariah 14:4), where He ascended into heaven after the resurrection (Acts 1:9–12). When this event occurs, every eye will see Jesus; the whole earth will witness the return of Jesus (Matthew 24, 30). When Jesus put His feet down at that time, He will reign as the King of all the earth (Zechariah 4:9). He is also returning as a judge to judge the dead and the living (John 5:26–29). At this time, the unbelievers are punished (2 Thessalonians 1:7–9). The Lord will stop the works of the Antichrist. How the Lord will fight is written in detail in the book of Revelation, the last chapter of the New Testament in the Bible. The fight between God and the Beast or evil forces is called "Armageddon" (Revelation 16:12–16). The second coming of Christ has been described as the Battle of Armageddon.

At the war's end, the Antichrist and the false prophet will be cast into the lake of fire (Revelation 19:20), Satan will be bound for a thousand years, and the saints will reign with Christ for a thousand years (Revelation 20:1–6). This setup of a thousand years is called the New Millennium. The Lord reigns on earth; He is called the King of Kings and the Lord of Lords (Zechariah 14:9, Revelation 19:11–21). Satan cannot do anything to the saints because he is bound for a thousand years. After a thousand years, Satan will be released for a while. In Revelation 20:7–10, the Bible states:

> When the thousand years have passed, Satan will be released from prison and go out to deceive the nations in the earth's four corners, Gog and Magog, to gather

them together to battle, whose number is the sand of the sea. They went up on the breadth of the earth and surrounded the camp of the saints and the beloved city. And fire came down from God out of heaven and devoured them. The devil, who deceived them, was cast into the lake of fire and brimstone where the beast and the false prophet are. And they will be tormented day and night forever and ever.

The devil will face a final battle with the Lord Almighty at this time. He will be thrown into hell forever and ever, together with the people who followed him. The devil is the defeated being at the end and stands no more change after the final war with God. In Revelation 20:11–15, the scripture conveys, "Then I saw a great white throne and Him who sat on it, from whose face the earth and the heaven fled away. And there was found no place for them. And I saw the dead, small and great, standing before God, and books were opened. And another book was opened, which is the Book of Life. And the dead were judged according to their works, by the things written in the books. The sea gave up the dead who were in it, and Death and Hades delivered up the dead who were in them. And they were judged, each one according to his works. Then Death and Hades were cast into the lake of fire. This is the second death. And anyone not found written in the Book of Life was cast into the lake of fire."

The second death is a final destiny for the unbelievers and the devil (Revelation 20:10). The Book of Life will be opened; in that book, everything was recorded. The dead will be judged according to the recorded works, and anyone's name not found in the book will be tossed into the lake of fire and spend an eternity there. On the other hand, the born-again faithful ones will be with God in New Heaven and New Earth (Revelation 21:1). This new creation is also called the New Jerusalem (Revelation 21:2). Why is it called new? Because the current world that we live in is subject to God's curse due to humanity's sin (Romans 8:19–22).

Heaven and earth will pass away (Mark 13:31), and it will be replaced with a new one (Revelation 21:5). In this new place, there will be no more pain, crying, and deaths (Revelation 21:4). Why no more sufferings? Because it is a world without the curse of sin (Revelation 22:3). God Himself will dwell with His people on the new glorious earth (Revelation 21:3). People of God or the believers will be in the dwelling place of God forever and ever. I encourage you to read the book of Revelation about the glorious place, where the everlasting beauty of God shines. This book's final chapter may seem complicated, and I don't deny that the book of Revelation may be a little challenging to understand, but continue your study to grasp a more profound knowledge of Christian eschatology. The question is, is your name written in that Book of Life? Are you going to be resurrected after death like Jesus was resurrected? If you are concerned about your eternal future, wonder who Jesus is, why He did what He did by hanging on the cross, what is sin and righteousness all about, or even don't have a clue about life on earth, you are confused, have no direction in life, well, there is hope. You have hope because an actual living God will shine the light to show you the way and keep you safe in His hands, up to the end into the New Heaven and New Earth. Below is the salvation prayer you can say aloud:

> "Lord, I know that I am a sinner. I confess all my sins. Please forgive me for my sins and iniquities. I believe you died on the cross for my sins and rose again on the third day from the dead. I turn away from my past and want to walk with you. Lord, please come into my heart. You are my Savior and my God. Holy Spirit, I ask you to lead me into the powerful life as a Christ believer."

Get into a Bible-believing church to grow in your faith. Read the Bible, and ask the Holy Spirit to teach you and give you understanding. Attend Bible study in your church, and surround yourself with born-again Bible-believer brothers and sisters in Christ, because iron sharpens iron (Proverbs 27:17).

God knows the end from the beginning (Isaiah 46:10), but we don't. Hence, hold on to the infallible Word of God in the Bible because it is a book of prophecy. Many events came to pass from the Old Testament into the New Testament. The final chapter of this book is about the power of the resurrection; it seems to be the end for us after we are resurrected like Jesus did (Isaiah 26:19, Job 19:26) because we will be with Jesus. Nevertheless, we must also know what happens to us beyond the resurrection. What a life we have in the hands of the living God. He is the author and finisher of our faith (Hebrews 12:2), Alpha and Omega, and ultimately the First and the Last (Revelation 22:13). His power is the everlasting power, and whoever belongs to Him lives in the power of Him Who created all things with eternal life covered in His love and majesty.

Conclusion

God is all-powerful, all-knowing, and all-present. Knowing these attributes of God is great; in other words, having the knowledge about God is wonderful, but Jesus is the God Who lives with His people in their hearts. He is a living God actively involved in a relationship with anyone who seeks Him. The Word of God in Jeremiah 29:13 says, "And you will seek Me and find Me when you search for Me with all your heart." Meanwhile, in 1 Chronicle 28:9, the Bible says, "As for you, my son Solomon, know the God of your father, and serve Him with a loyal heart and with a willing mind; for the Lord searches all hearts and understands all the intent of the thoughts. If you seek Him, He will be found by you; but if you forsake Him, He will cast you off forever."

Having a relationship with Jesus means we are equipped to face every challenge in this world with the power of the almighty God. From the moment of our salvation, God never stops working with us. He starts to transform our lives, give us the desire to read the Word of God, build our faith, put us in the blood covenant with Him, give us spiritual gifts to help others, separate us from the evil ones or the darkness of the world, allowing us to experience His tangible presence and finally resurrect our physical body after death. This is called a powerful life in the hands of a powerful Jesus. Jesus is Lord, and the world is in His hands; a wise man will choose the almighty God to bring life to a fruitful completion. He who has begun a good work in you will complete it until the day of Jesus Christ (Philippians 1:6).

May the Lord bless you and keep you. Amen.

Printed in the United States
by Baker & Taylor Publisher Services